Mastering Sales: Strategies for Winning Deals

Asit Saha

Published by Asit Saha, 2024.

While every precaution has been taken in the preparation of this book, the publisher assumes no responsibility for errors or omissions, or for damages resulting from the use of the information contained herein.

MASTERING SALES: STRATEGIES FOR WINNING DEALS

First edition. March 24, 2024.

ISBN: 979-8224724949

Written by Asit Saha.

Overview: "Mastering Sales: Strategies for Winning Deals"

In "Mastering Sales: Strategies for Winning Deals," readers embark on a transformative journey to become true masters of the sales craft. This comprehensive guide is designed to equip sales professionals with the knowledge, skills, and strategies needed to consistently secure successful deals and achieve sales excellence in today's competitive marketplace.

Key Themes and Focus Areas:

Foundations of Sales Excellence: The book begins by laying a solid foundation for sales mastery, exploring fundamental principles such as understanding customer needs, effective communication, and building trust and rapport.

Navigating the Sales Process:

Readers are guided through each stage of the sales process, from prospecting and lead generation to negotiation and closing. Practical strategies and techniques are provided to help navigate common challenges and obstacles encountered along the way.

Strategic Selling Techniques:

Emphasizing the importance of strategic selling, the book delves into advanced techniques for identifying and qualifying leads, uncovering customer pain points, and tailoring solutions to meet specific needs.

Overcoming Objections and Closing Deals:

Readers learn how to effectively overcome objections, handle rejections, and navigate the closing process with confidence and finesse. Proven strategies for overcoming common objections and securing commitment are explored in detail.

Negotiation and Relationship Building: Negotiation is a critical aspect of the sales process, and readers are provided with practical tips and techniques for negotiating win-win outcomes and building long-term relationships with clients.

Continuous Learning and Improvement: Central to the book's philosophy is the idea of continuous learning and improvement. Readers are encouraged to adopt a growth mindset, seek out new knowledge and skills, and continually refine their approach to sales.

Unique Features:

Real-World Case Studies: Throughout the book, readers encounter real-world case studies and examples that illustrate key concepts and demonstrate how they can be applied in practice.

Actionable Insights:

Each chapter includes actionable insights to help readers reinforce their learning, apply new techniques, and track their progress.

Expert Advice and Tips:

Drawing on the expertise of seasoned sales professionals, the book offers valuable advice, tips, and best practices to inspire and empower readers on their sales journey.

Target Audience:

"Mastering Sales: Strategies for Winning Deals" is designed for sales professionals at all levels, from newcomers looking to establish a solid foundation to seasoned veterans seeking to refine their skills and take their sales performance to the next level. Additionally, entrepreneurs, business owners, and anyone involved in marketing or business development will find valuable insights to enhance their sales efforts.

"Mastering Sales: Strategies for Winning Deals" is a comprehensive guide and indispensable resource for anyone seeking to achieve mastery in the art of sales. Packed with practical strategies, actionable techniques, and expert advice, this book empowers readers to unlock their full potential, secure winning deals, and achieve unparalleled success in the competitive world of sales.

Table of Contents

Introduction:

Chapter 1: Understanding the Sales Process

Introduction:

The importance of effective sales techniques cannot be overstated in today's competitive business landscape. In a world where consumers are bombarded with choices and information overload, the ability to stand out and connect with potential buyers is crucial for success. Effective sales techniques not only help in closing deals but also in building long-lasting relationships with customers.

One of the primary benefits of mastering sales techniques is the ability to understand and address the needs of customers. By employing active listening skills and asking the right questions, sales professionals can uncover the pain points and challenges faced by potential buyers. This understanding allows them to tailor their offerings to meet the specific needs of each individual customer, increasing the likelihood of a successful sale.

Furthermore, effective sales techniques play an imperative role in building trust and credibility with customers. In an era where skepticism towards traditional advertising is on the rise, consumers are more likely to trust recommendations from people they perceive as credible and trustworthy. By demonstrating expertise, providing valuable insights, and offering genuine solutions to customer problems, sales professionals can earn the trust and respect of their clients, paving the way for future business opportunities.

Moreover, mastering sales techniques empowers sales professionals to navigate the complexities of the negotiation process with confidence. Whether it's overcoming objections, negotiating terms, or handling difficult conversations, having a solid foundation in sales techniques can make the difference between success and failure. By understanding the value proposition and effectively communicating the benefits of their offerings, sales professionals can persuade prospects to make purchasing decisions that are mutually beneficial.

In addition to closing deals, effective sales techniques also contribute to the overall success and growth of a business. By consistently delivering exceptional customer experiences and generating positive word-of-mouth referrals, sales professionals can help drive revenue and expand the customer base. Furthermore, by staying informed about industry trends and market dynamics, sales professionals can identify new opportunities for growth and adapt their strategies accordingly.

Chapter 1: Understanding the Sales Process

Understanding the sales process is fundamental for anyone aiming to excel in sales. It's not just about selling a product or service; it's about guiding potential customers through a journey that leads to a triumphant transaction. Here's a breakdown of the key components involved:

Prospecting and Lead Generation:

The sales process often begins with prospecting, which involves identifying potential customers who might have a need or interest in what you're offering.

Lead generation tactics can include networking, cold calling, email outreach, social media engagement, and more.

Qualifying Leads:

Not all leads are created equal. It's essential to qualify leads to determine if they have the budget, authority, need, and timeline (BANT) to make a purchase.

This step helps prioritize efforts and focus on leads with the highest likelihood of conversion.

Research and Preparation:

Before engaging with a prospect, it's crucial to carry out thorough research to understand their business, industry, pain points, and any potential challenges they may be facing.

Preparation involves crafting a tailored approach and solution that aligns with the prospect's needs and objectives.

Initiating Contact:

Once qualified leads have been identified and researched, it's time to make initial contact. This can be done through various channels, such as phone calls, emails, social media messages, or in-person meetings.

The goal is to establish rapport and begin building a relationship with the prospect.

Discovery and Needs Analysis:

During the sales conversation, the focus shifts to understanding the prospect's challenges, goals, and pain points.

Asking open-ended questions and actively listening to the prospect's responses are essential for uncovering their needs and determining how your product or service can provide value.

Presenting Solutions:

Based on the information gathered during the discovery phase, it's time to present tailored solutions that address the prospect's specific needs and objectives.

This involves highlighting the features and benefits of your offering and demonstrating how it can solve the prospect's problems or help achieve their goals.

Handling Objections:

It's common for prospects to raise objections or concerns during the sales process. Effective sales professionals anticipate these objections and are prepared to address them with confidence and empathy.

By understanding the prospect's underlying motivations and objections, sales professionals can overcome resistance and move the conversation forward.

Closing the Sale:

The culmination of the sales process is the closing stage, where the prospect makes the decision to purchase.

This involves asking for the sale in a clear and confident manner, addressing any remaining concerns, and guiding the prospect through the final steps of the transaction.

Follow-Up and Relationship Building:

The sales process doesn't end once the deal is closed. Follow-up is crucial for ensuring customer satisfaction, addressing any post-sale issues, and nurturing long-term relationships.

Building strong relationships with customers can lead to repeat business, referrals, and opportunities for up-selling or cross-selling in the future.

Identifying and qualifying leads

Identifying and qualifying leads is a vital aspect of the sales process, as it sets the foundation for successful interactions and conversions. Here's an in-depth look at each component:

1. *Identifying Leads:*

Market Research: Start by conducting thorough market research to identify potential customers who fit your target demographic. Understand their needs, pain points, and preferences.

Networking: Attend industry events, join relevant online forums and groups, and engage in networking activities to connect with potential leads. Networking helps to expand your reach and identify prospects who may be interested in your offerings.

Inbound Marketing: Utilize inbound marketing tactics such as content creation, search engine optimization (SEO), social media marketing, and email campaigns to attract leads who are actively seeking solutions that you offer.

Referrals: Leverage existing relationships with satisfied customers, partners, and colleagues to obtain referrals. Referrals are often high-quality leads as they come with a level of trust already established.

Lead Generation Tools: Explore various lead generation tools and platforms such as lead capture forms on your website, CRM systems, and lead databases to identify potential prospects.

2. *Qualifying Leads:*

Budget: Find out if the lead has the financial resources to invest in your product or service. Understanding their budget constraints early on helps prioritize efforts and focus on leads with genuine potential.

Authority: Identify whether the lead has the decision-making authority within their organization. Dealing with decision-makers streamlines the sales process and reduces the likelihood of encountering roadblocks during negotiations.

Need: Assess whether the lead has a genuine need or pain point that your product or service can address. Understanding their specific challenges allows you to tailor your solution and value proposition accordingly.

Timeline: Determine the lead's timeline for making a purchase decision. Some leads may have an urgent need, while others may be exploring options for the future. Aligning your sales efforts with the lead's timeline increases the likelihood of conversion.

Fit: Evaluate whether your offering aligns with the lead's requirements, objectives, and preferences. Not every lead will be an ideal fit for your product or service, and it's essential to focus on those prospects who are most likely to benefit from what you offer.

3. Lead Scoring:

Consider implementing a lead scoring system to prioritize leads based on their likelihood of conversion. Assign numerical values to various criteria such as demographics, engagement level, and behavior, and use this scoring system to identify and focus on high-potential leads.

Regularly review and update your lead scoring criteria to ensure relevance and accuracy. As leads progress through the sales funnel, their scores may change based on new information or interactions.

Importance of research and preparation

The importance of research and preparation in the sales process cannot be overstated. It serves as the foundation upon which successful sales interactions are built, enabling sales professionals to understand their prospects, tailor their approach, and ultimately increase their chances of closing deals. Here's why research and preparation are crucial:

1. *Understanding the Prospect:*

Identifying Needs and Pain Points:

Research allows sales professionals to gather insights into the prospect's industry, company, and specific challenges they may be facing.

This understanding enables them to position their product or service as a solution to the prospect's needs and pain points.

Building Rapport:

By conducting research on the prospect's background, interests, and professional history, sales professionals can find common ground and establish relationship more effectively. This helps create a connection and builds trust, making the sales conversation more productive.

2. *Tailoring the Approach:*

Customizing Solutions: Armed with information gathered through research, sales professionals can tailor their approach and offerings to align with the prospect's unique requirements and objectives. This personalized approach demonstrates a genuine understanding of the prospect's needs and increases the likelihood of a positive response.

Anticipating Objections: Research allows sales professionals to anticipate potential objections or concerns that the prospect may raise during the sales conversation. By addressing these objections proactively and offering relevant information or solutions, sales professionals can overcome resistance and move the conversation forward.

3. *Enhancing Credibility:*

Demonstrating Expertise:

Thorough research enables sales professionals to demonstrate their expertise and industry knowledge during interactions with prospects. This positions them as trusted advisors rather than just salespeople, enhancing their credibility and authority in the eyes of the prospect.

Providing Value:

By providing valuable insights, data, and recommendations based on research findings, sales professionals can showcase the value they bring to the table. This creates a positive impression and fosters confidence in the prospect's mind, making them more receptive to the sales pitch.

4. Maximizing Efficiency:

Prioritizing Efforts:

Research helps sales professionals prioritize their efforts by focusing on leads with the highest potential for conversion. By identifying prospects who align with their ideal customer profile and have a genuine need for their offering, sales professionals can allocate their time and resources more efficiently.

Avoiding Wasted Opportunities:

Without proper research, sales professionals risk engaging with prospects who are not good fits for their product or service. By conducting thorough research upfront, they can avoid wasted opportunities and instead concentrate on prospects that are more likely to convert.

Chapter 2: Building Strong Relationships

Developing relationship with clients is a cornerstone of successful sales interactions. It lays the groundwork for trust, understanding, and mutual respect, ultimately fostering long-lasting relationships. Here are key reasons why developing rapport is crucial in sales:

1. *Establishing Trust:*

Trust is essential in any business relationship, and developing rapport is the first step toward earning a client's trust.

Building rapport involves creating a connection based on shared interests, values, or experiences, which helps alleviate the client's apprehensions and concerns.

2. *Creating a Positive Atmosphere:*

A strong rapport creates a positive and comfortable atmosphere during sales interactions, making clients feel at ease and open to communication.

Clients are more likely to engage with a sales professional who they perceive as friendly, approachable, and genuinely interested in their needs.

3. *Enhancing Communication:*

Developing rapport facilitates effective communication by encouraging open dialogue and active listening.

Sales professionals who have established rapport with clients are better able to understand their needs, preferences, and concerns, leading to more productive conversations and tailored solutions.

4. *Building Credibility:*

Rapport-building demonstrates professionalism and sincerity, enhancing the sales professional's credibility in the eyes of the client.

Clients are more inclined to trust and value recommendations from sales professionals with whom they have a strong rapport.

5. *Strengthening Relationships:*

Beyond individual transactions, developing rapport fosters long-term relationships with clients.

Clients are more likely to remain loyal and continue doing business with sales professionals whom they trust and feel comfortable with.

6. *Overcoming Objections:*

A solid rapport can help sales professionals navigate objections more effectively. Clients who maintain a positive relationship with a sales professional are more likely to be receptive to constructive feedback and willing to consider alternative solutions.

7. *Personalizing Solutions:*

When clients feel valued and understood, sales professionals can tailor solutions to better meet their specific needs and preferences.

By taking the time to develop rapport, sales professionals gain insights into the client's goals, challenges, and motivations, allowing them to offer personalized recommendations.

8. *Differentiating from Competitors:*

In a competitive marketplace, building strong rapport with clients can be a key differentiator.

Clients are more likely to choose to do business with sales professionals whom they feel genuinely care about their success and well-being.

Effective communication skills

Effective communication skills are paramount for sales professionals as they form the backbone of successful interactions with clients. From building rapport to conveying value propositions, mastering communication techniques is essential for driving sales. Here are key aspects of effective communication skills:

1. *Active Listening:*

Active listening involves fully concentrating, understanding, responding, and remembering what the client is saying.

Sales professionals should listen attentively to clients' needs, concerns, and preferences to demonstrate empathy and understanding.

2. *Clarity and Conciseness:*

Communicating clearly and concisely ensures that the message is easily understood by the client.

Sales professionals should avoid jargon and use simple language to articulate their points effectively.

3. *Asking Open-Ended Questions:*

Open-ended questions encourage clients to provide detailed responses, leading to a deeper understanding of their needs and motivations.

Sales professionals should use open-ended questions to uncover valuable insights and engage clients in meaningful conversations.

4. *Empathy and Understanding:*

Demonstrating empathy and understanding helps build rapport and trust with clients.

Sales professionals should put themselves in the client's shoes, acknowledging their challenges and showing genuine concern for their well-being.

5. *Nonverbal Communication:*

Nonverbal cues such as facial expressions, body language, and tone of voice play a significant role in communication.

Sales professionals should maintain positive body language, make eye contact, and convey confidence and enthusiasm through their tone of voice.

6. *Tailoring Communication Styles:*

Adapting communication styles to go with the preferences and personality of the client enhances engagement and rapport.

Sales professionals should observe and adjust their communication approach based on the client's communication style, whether it's analytical, expressive, amiable, or assertive.

7. *Building Rapport:*

Building rapport involves establishing a connection and fostering trust and mutual respect with clients.

Sales professionals should show genuine interest in the client, ask about their interests and experiences, and find common ground to create a positive relationship.

8. *Handling Objections Effectively:*

Effective communication skills are crucial for addressing client objections and concerns.

Sales professionals should listen actively, acknowledge the client's concerns, provide relevant information or solutions, and guide the conversation toward a positive resolution.

9. *Following Up:*

Clear and timely communication during follow-up interactions reinforces trust and demonstrates commitment to the client. Sales professionals should communicate proactively, providing updates, addressing any post-sale issues, and expressing gratitude for the client's business.

Building trust and credibility

Building trust and credibility is crucial for sales professionals as it forms the foundation of successful relationships with clients. Trust and credibility are the cornerstones upon which clients base their decisions to engage in business transactions. Here are a few tricks sales professionals can follow to build trust and credibility:

1. *Consistency and Reliability:*

Consistently delivering on promises and commitments helps establish trust with clients.

Sales professionals should strive to meet deadlines, deliver quality products or services, and provide reliable support to build a reputation for reliability.

2. *Transparency and Honesty:*

Transparency and truthfulness are essential for building trust and credibility.

Sales professionals should be upfront about limitations, potential risks, and challenges associated with their offerings, avoiding exaggerations or misleading claims.

3. *Expertise and Knowledge:*

Demonstrating expertise and industry knowledge instills confidence in clients. Sales professionals should stay informed about industry trends, regulations, and best practices, positioning themselves as trusted advisors who can provide valuable insights and recommendations.

4. *Listening and Understanding:*

Actively listening to clients and understanding their needs and concerns fosters trust and empathy.

Sales professionals should listen attentively, ask probing questions, and demonstrate genuine concern for the client's success.

5. *Providing Value:*

Offering value-added solutions and going above and beyond to meet client needs builds credibility. Sales professionals should focus on providing solutions that genuinely benefit the client, even if it means recommending alternative options or customizing offerings to align with their requirements.

6. Building Relationships:

Building strong, long-term relationships with clients is the gateway to establishing trust and credibility. Sales professionals should invest time in getting to know clients on a personal level, nurturing relationships beyond individual transactions, and demonstrating a genuine interest in their success.

7. *Testimonials and References:*

Positive testimonials and references from satisfied clients serve as social proof of a sales professional's credibility. Sales professionals should proactively collect and showcase testimonials and references to validate their track record and reassure potential clients of their capabilities.

8. *Handling Challenges Gracefully:*

How sales professionals handle challenges and setbacks can significantly impact their credibility. Sales professionals should approach challenges with professionalism, honesty, and a commitment to finding solutions, demonstrating resilience and integrity in the face of adversity.

9. *Follow-Up and Support:*

Providing exceptional post-sale support and follow-up demonstrates a commitment to the client's satisfaction and success. Sales professionals should proactively communicate with clients, address any post-sale issues promptly, and offer ongoing support to build trust and loyalty.

Chapter 3: Identifying Customer Needs

Active listening is a fundamental skill for sales professionals as it enables them to understand their clients' needs, concerns, and preferences more deeply. By actively listening, sales professionals can build rapport, demonstrate empathy, and tailor their approach to meet the client's specific requirements. Here are key active listening techniques that sales professionals can employ:

1. *Give Undivided Attention:*

Focus entirely on the client and avoid distractions such as phones, emails, or other interruptions.

Maintain eye contact and use nonverbal cues to convey interest and attentiveness.

2. *Listen Without Interrupting*:

Resist the urge to interrupt or interject while the client is speaking.

Allow the client to express themselves fully before responding, showing respect for their perspective and opinions.

3. *Use Verbal Cues:*

Encourage the client to continue speaking with verbal cues such as "I see," "Go on," or "Tell me more."

Use affirmations and acknowledgments to signal that you are actively engaged in the conversation.

4. *Paraphrase and Summarize:*

Paraphrase the client's statements to demonstrate understanding and clarify any points of confusion.

Summarize key points periodically to ensure alignment and capture the essence of the conversation.

5. *Ask Clarifying Questions:*

Ask open-ended questions to delve deeper into the client's thoughts, feelings, and motivations.

Seek clarification on any ambiguous or unclear statements to ensure a complete understanding of the client's needs.

6. *Reflect Emotions:*

Recognize and reflect the client's emotions, validating their feelings and demonstrating empathy.

Mirror the client's tone and emotion to establish rapport and create a connection.

7. *Listen for Nonverbal Cues:*

Pay attention to nonverbal cues such as facial expressions, body language, and tone of voice.

Interpret nonverbal cues to gain insights into the client's emotions, preferences, and level of engagement.

8. *Respond Appropriately:*

Respond thoughtfully and empathetically to the client's concerns and questions.

Tailor your responses to address the client's specific needs and provide relevant information or solutions.

9. *Avoid Prejudgment:*

Suspend judgment and avoid making assumptions about the client's intentions or motivations.

Approach each interaction with an open mind and a willingness to listen without bias.

10. *Practice Empathy:*

Put yourself in the client's shoes and try to understand their perspective and experiences.

Show empathy by acknowledging their feelings and demonstrating genuine concern for their well-being.

Asking Probing Questions

Asking probing questions is a powerful technique that sales professionals use to uncover valuable insights, understand client needs, and guide the sales conversation towards a successful outcome. Probing questions delve deeper into the client's challenges, goals, and motivations, facilitating a more meaningful and productive interaction.

These are the ways sales professionals can effectively utilize probing questions:

1. Clarify Understanding:

Begin by asking open-ended questions to encourage the client to share their thoughts and experiences.

Follow up with probing questions to clarify any ambiguous or vague responses, ensuring a complete understanding of the client's situation.

2. Uncover Pain Points:

Probe to uncover the client's pain points, challenges, and areas of dissatisfaction.

Ask questions that explore the root causes of their problems and the impact they have on their business or personal life.

3. Identify Needs and Objectives:

Probe to identify the client's needs, objectives, and desired outcomes.

Ask questions that reveal the client's goals, priorities, and expectations for the solution they are seeking.

4. Explore Budget and Timeline:

Probe to understand the client's budget constraints and timeline for making a decision.

Ask questions that uncover the client's financial considerations, purchasing process, and deadlines.

5. Assess Decision-Making Process:

Probe to gain insights into the client's decision-making process and key decision-makers involved.

Ask questions that reveal the client's decision criteria, evaluation criteria, and any internal approval processes.

6. Uncover Competitive Landscape:

Probe to understand the client's perception of competing solutions or alternatives.

Ask questions that explore the client's experiences with other providers, their likes and dislikes, and their criteria for comparison.

7. Address Objections and Concerns:

Probe to uncover any objections or concerns the client may have about moving forward.

Ask questions that explore the underlying reasons for their objections and address any misconceptions or uncertainties.

8. Customize Solutions:

Probe to gather information that enables you to tailor your solution to meet the client's specific needs.

Ask questions that reveal the client's preferences, requirements, and desired features or functionalities.

9. Build Rapport and Trust:

Use probing questions as an opportunity to demonstrate empathy, understanding, and genuine interest in the client's success.

Ask questions that show you are actively listening and deeply invested in finding the best possible solution for the client.

10. Guide the Conversation:

Use probing questions strategically to guide the conversation towards a mutually beneficial outcome.

Ask questions that help uncover areas of alignment between your offering and the client's needs, positioning your solution as the ideal choice.

Understanding pain points and challenges

Understanding pain points and challenges is essential for sales professionals as it allows them to tailor their approach and solutions to effectively address the needs of their clients. Pain points refer to specific problems, frustrations, or obstacles that clients encounter in their business or personal lives. By identifying and empathizing with these pain points, sales professionals can position their products or services as solutions that alleviate these challenges. With these tricks, sales professionals can understand and address client pain points effectively:

1. Deploy Active Listening:

Actively listen to clients during conversations to identify and understand their pain points.

Pay attention to verbal cues, such as complaints, frustrations, or challenges mentioned by the client.

2. Ask Probing Questions:

Ask open-ended and probing questions to delve deeper into the client's challenges and pain points.

Encourage the client to elaborate on specific issues they are facing and how these challenges impact their business or personal objectives.

3. Empathize with the Client:

Demonstrate empathy and understanding towards the client's pain points and challenges.

Put yourself in the client's shoes and acknowledge the difficulties they are experiencing.

4. Research the Client's Industry and Market:

Conduct research to gain insights into the client's industry, market trends, and competitive landscape.

Understand the common pain points and challenges faced by clients in similar industries or sectors.

5. Prioritize Pain Points:

Prioritize pain points based on their severity, impact, and urgency for the client.

Focus on addressing the most critical pain points that have the greatest potential to drive value for the client.

6. Offer Solutions and Benefits:

Tailor your solutions to directly address the client's pain points and challenges.

Highlight the specific benefits and advantages of your product or service in alleviating these pain points.

7. Provide Case Studies and Success Stories:

Share case studies and success stories of how your solutions have helped other clients overcome similar pain points.

Use real-world examples to demonstrate the effectiveness of your offerings in addressing client challenges.

8. Collaborate with the Client:

Collaborate with the client to brainstorm potential solutions and strategies for overcoming their pain points.

Involve the client in the decision-making process and seek their input and feedback on proposed solutions.

9. Anticipate Future Pain Points:

Anticipate potential future pain points and challenges that the client may encounter.

Proactively offer solutions and recommendations to prevent or mitigate these challenges before they arise.

10. Follow-Up and Support:

Follow up with the client after the sale to ensure that their pain points have been effectively addressed.

Provide ongoing support and assistance to the client to ensure their continued success and satisfaction.

Chapter 4: Presenting Solutions

Tailoring solutions to customer needs is a cornerstone of successful sales. It involves understanding the unique requirements, preferences, and objectives of each customer and customizing offerings accordingly. By aligning solutions with customer needs, sales professionals can demonstrate value, increase customer satisfaction, and differentiate themselves from competitors. This is how sales professionals can effectively tailor solutions to customer needs:

1. Active Listening and Discovery:

Begin by actively listening to the customer to understand their challenges, goals, and priorities.

Use probing questions and discovery techniques to uncover specific needs and preferences.

2. Customize Offerings:

Customize your products or services to meet the unique requirements of the customer.

Offer customization options, add-on features, or flexible pricing plans to accommodate their needs.

3. Highlight Relevant Features and Benefits:

Emphasize the features and benefits of your offerings that are most relevant to the customer's needs and objectives.

Explain how your solution addresses their specific pain points and helps achieve their desired outcomes.

4. Provide Value Propositions:

Clearly articulate the value proposition of your solution in relation to the customer's needs.

Highlight how your offering provides tangible benefits and ROI that align with the customer's goals.

5. Offer Personalized Recommendations:

Provide personalized recommendations based on the customer's unique situation and preferences.

Suggest solutions that are tailored to their industry, size, budget, and other relevant factors.

6. Adapt Communication Style:

Adapt your communication style to match the preferences of the customer.

Tailor your messaging and presentation to resonate with their language, tone, and communication preferences.

7. Address Concerns and Objections:

Anticipate and address any concerns or objections the customer may have about your solution.

Provide evidence, testimonials, or case studies to reassure them and demonstrate the effectiveness of your offering.

8. Collaborate with the Customer:

Involve the customer in the decision-making process and seek their input and feedback.

Collaborate on co-creating solutions that meet their needs and align with their vision.

9. Follow-Up and Support:

Follow up with the customer after the sale to ensure their satisfaction and address any additional needs.

Provide ongoing support, training, and assistance to help them maximize the value of your solution.

10. Continuously Improve and Adapt:

Gather feedback from customers to identify areas for improvement and innovation.

Continuously adapt your offerings and services to evolve with changing customer needs and market trends.

Highlighting product or service benefits

Highlighting product or service benefits is essential in sales as it helps customers understand the value and relevance of what you're offering to their specific needs and challenges. Focusing on benefits rather than just features can make your offerings more compelling and persuasive. Here's how to effectively highlight the benefits of your product or service:

1. Identify Key Benefits:

Begin by identifying the primary benefits of your product or service. These are the outcomes or advantages that customers will experience by using your offering.

2. Understand Customer Needs:

Tailor your messaging to address specific pain points and challenges that your customers face. Understanding their needs allows you to position your benefits more effectively.

3. Focus on Solutions:

Frame the benefits of your product or service as solutions to customer problems. Emphasize how your offering can help customers overcome challenges and achieve their goals.

4. Use Clear and Concise Language:

Clearly communicate the benefits using simple and straightforward language. Avoid technical jargon or industry-specific terms that may confuse or overwhelm customers.

5. Provide Tangible Examples:

Illustrate the benefits with real-life examples or case studies that demonstrate how your offering has helped other customers. Concrete examples make the benefits more tangible and relatable.

6. Quantify the Benefits:

Whenever possible, quantify the benefits in terms of time saved, cost reduction, revenue increase, or other measurable outcomes. This adds credibility and makes the benefits more compelling.

7. Prioritize Benefits:

Prioritize the most impactful benefits and lead with them in your messaging. Focus on benefits that are most relevant to the customer's needs and objectives.

8. Address Objections:

Anticipate potential objections or concerns that customers may have about your offering and proactively address them. Explain how the benefits outweigh any perceived drawbacks or risks.

9. Tailor Benefits to Different Audiences:

Customize your messaging to highlight benefits that resonate with different customer segments or personas. Consider the unique needs and preferences of each audience when communicating benefits.

10. Reinforce Benefits Throughout the Sales Process:

Continuously reinforce the benefits of your offering throughout the sales process, from initial contact to closing the sale. Consistent messaging helps customers understand and remember the value proposition.

11. Provide Social Proof:

Use testimonials, reviews, or endorsements from satisfied customers to reinforce the benefits of your offering. Social proof builds credibility and validates the effectiveness of your solution.

Overcoming objections effectively

Overcoming objections effectively is a critical skill in sales that separates successful sales professionals from the rest. Objections are a natural part of the sales process and can arise due to various reasons, including price concerns, skepticism about the product or service, or uncertainty about the value proposition. These tricks can help overcome objections effectively:

1. Anticipate Objections:

Prepare in advance by identifying common objections that customers may raise during the sales process.

Anticipating objections allows you to formulate responses and strategies to address them proactively.

2. Active Listening:

Listen carefully to the customer's objections without interrupting or becoming defensive.

Demonstrate empathy and understanding by acknowledging the validity of their concerns.

3. Clarify Objections:

Ask clarifying questions to gain a deeper understanding of the customer's objections.

Seek to uncover the underlying reasons behind their concerns and address them directly.

4. Reframe the Objection:

Reframe the objection in a positive light and highlight alternative perspectives or solutions.

Help the customer see the objection as an opportunity for discussion rather than a barrier to making a purchase.

5. Provide Relevant Information:

Offer factual information, data, or evidence to support your response to the objection.

Share case studies, testimonials, or success stories that demonstrate the effectiveness of your product or service in addressing similar concerns.

6. Address Value Proposition:

Reinforce the value proposition of your offering and emphasize the benefits that the customer will receive.

Clearly articulate how your product or service addresses the customer's needs and solves their problems.

7. Handle Objections with Confidence:

Respond to objections with confidence and professionalism, demonstrating your expertise and credibility.

Avoid becoming defensive or argumentative, and remain calm and composed throughout the interaction.

8. Offer Solutions:

Propose solutions or alternatives to address the customer's objections and alleviate their concerns.

Tailor your responses to meet the specific needs and preferences of the customer.

9. Close with a Trial Close:

After addressing the objection, use a trial close to measure the customer's receptiveness to moving forward.

Ask questions to confirm that the objection has been effectively resolved and to encourage the customer to take the next step.

10. Follow-Up and Reassure:

Follow up with the customer after the objection has been addressed to ensure their satisfaction.

Reassure the customer of your commitment to their success and offer ongoing support and assistance as needed.

Chapter 5: Negotiation Strategies

Understanding the value of sales negotiation is crucial for sales professionals as it allows them to navigate complex situations, overcome objections, and secure favorable outcomes for both parties involved. Sales negotiation is more than just haggling over prices; it's about finding mutually beneficial solutions that address the needs and interests of both the buyer and the seller. Here's why sales negotiation is valuable:

1. Maximizing Value:

Sales negotiation enables both parties to maximize the value they receive from the transaction.

By exploring different options and concessions, sales professionals can identify opportunities to create additional value for the customer while still achieving their own objectives.

2. Building Relationships:

Negotiation provides an opportunity to build trust, rapport, and understanding between the buyer and the seller.

Through open dialogue and collaborative problem-solving, sales professionals can strengthen relationships with customers and lay the foundation for long-term partnerships.

3. Addressing Complex Needs:

Many sales transactions involve complex needs, requirements, and constraints that cannot be addressed through a one-size-fits-all approach.

Negotiation allows sales professionals to tailor solutions to meet the unique circumstances and preferences of each customer, leading to more satisfied clients and higher success rates.

4. Overcoming Objections:

Sales negotiation provides a forum for addressing objections and concerns raised by customers.

By actively listening, empathizing, and providing solutions, sales professionals can overcome objections and build confidence in their offerings.

5. Creating Win-Win Outcomes:

Successful negotiation results in win-win outcomes where both parties feel satisfied with the terms of the agreement.

By finding common ground and balancing interests, sales professionals can create value for both the customer and the organization.

6. Differentiating from Competitors:

Effective negotiation skills can be a key differentiator in a competitive marketplace.

Sales professionals who can navigate negotiations successfully and deliver added value to customers are more likely to stand out from competitors and win business.

7. Increasing Profitability:

Negotiation allows sales professionals to capture additional value and increase profitability for their organization.

By negotiating favorable terms, pricing, and contract terms, sales professionals can improve the overall profitability of sales transactions.

8. Enhancing Problem-Solving Skills:

Negotiation provides an opportunity to hone problem-solving, critical thinking, and decision-making skills.

Sales professionals who excel at negotiation are better equipped to address complex challenges and adapt to changing circumstances in the sales process.

9. Driving Business Growth:

Effective negotiation contributes to business growth by securing new customers, expanding existing accounts, and increasing revenue.

By consistently achieving favorable outcomes in negotiations, sales professionals contribute to the overall success and growth of their organization.

Setting Stage for Negotiation

Setting the stage for successful negotiations is crucial for achieving mutually beneficial outcomes and building strong relationships with clients. It involves careful planning, communication, and preparation to create an environment conducive to productive discussions and positive results. Here's how to set the stage for successful negotiations:

1. Establish Objectives:

Clearly define your objectives and desired outcomes for the negotiation.

Set specific goals and benchmarks to measure success and guide your strategy.

2. Research and Preparation:

Conduct thorough research on the client, their needs, preferences, and industry trends.

Prepare a comprehensive understanding of your own position, strengths, weaknesses, and potential concessions.

3. Build Rapport:

Foster a positive relationship with the client based on trust, respect, and mutual understanding.

Invest time in building rapport before the negotiation to establish a foundation of goodwill.

4. Set the Agenda:

Outline the agenda for the negotiation and communicate it to the client in advance.

Clearly define the topics to be discussed, the objectives for each, and the expected outcomes.

5. Establish Ground Rules:

Agree on ground rules for the negotiation, including communication protocols, decision-making processes, and timelines.

Ensure that both parties understand and agree to the rules to facilitate a fair and transparent negotiation.

6. Focus on Interests, Not Positions:

Shift the focus from rigid positions to underlying interests and needs.

Encourage open dialogue and brainstorming to explore creative solutions that meet the interests of both parties.

7. Practice Active Listening:

Listen attentively to the client's concerns, priorities, and objectives.

Demonstrate empathy and understanding by acknowledging their perspective and validating their concerns.

8. Communicate Clearly and Effectively:

Use clear and concise language to convey your points and proposals.

Avoid ambiguity or misunderstandings by communicating openly and transparently.

9. Generate Options:

Generate a range of options and alternatives to address different scenarios and outcomes.

Encourage brainstorming and creative thinking to explore all possible solutions.

10. Manage Emotions:

Keep emotions in check and maintain a calm and composed demeanor throughout the negotiation.

Focus on facts and logic rather than allowing emotions to dictate the conversation.

11. Anticipate Objections and Responses:

Anticipate potential objections or challenges that may arise during the negotiation.

Prepare thoughtful responses and counterarguments to address objections effectively.

12. Seek Win-Win Solutions:

Make every effort for win-win outcomes that satisfy the interests of both parties.

Look for opportunities to create value and build long-term relationships rather than focusing solely on immediate gains.

13. Summarize and Confirm Agreement:

Summarize key points and agreements reached during the negotiation.

Confirm understanding and consensus to ensure clarity and alignment before concluding the negotiation.

Win-win negotiation techniques

Win-win negotiation techniques are essential for creating mutually beneficial outcomes where both parties feel satisfied with the terms of the agreement. These techniques focus on collaborative problem-solving, open communication, and creative solutions that address the interests and objectives of both sides. Here are some effective win-win negotiation techniques:

1. Identify Common Interests:

Begin by identifying shared interests and objectives that both parties have in common.

Focus on areas where there is potential for collaboration and mutual benefit.

2. Ask Open-Ended Questions:

Use open-ended questions to encourage dialogue and uncover the other party's underlying needs and motivations.

Seek to understand their priorities, concerns, and goals.

3. Active Listening:

Listen attentively to the other party's perspective without interrupting or judgment.

Demonstrate empathy and understanding by acknowledging their concerns and validating their viewpoints.

4. Brainstorm Solutions:

Collaborate with the other party to brainstorm creative solutions that address both sides' interests.

Encourage a free exchange of ideas and explore all possible options.

5. Prioritize Interests:

Prioritize interests based on their importance to each party and the potential for mutual gain.

Focus on finding solutions that satisfy the most critical interests for both sides.

6. Trade-offs and Concessions:

Be willing to make trade-offs and concessions to reach a mutually acceptable agreement.

Look for opportunities to give and take in areas where concessions are less costly or more valuable.

7. Expand the Pie:

Explore ways to expand the value or scope of the negotiation to create more opportunities for mutual gain.

Look for creative solutions that add value for both parties beyond the initial terms of the agreement.

8. Build Trust and Rapport:

Foster trust and rapport with the other party through transparent communication and integrity.

Demonstrate reliability and commitment to finding a solution that benefits both sides.

9. Use Objective Criteria:

Make decisions on objective criteria, such as market value, industry standards, or data-driven metrics.

Use objective criteria to guide negotiations and avoid getting bogged down in subjective arguments.

10. Focus on Long-Term Relationships:

Prioritize building long-term relationships over short-term gains.

Consider the potential impact of the negotiation on future interactions and the overall relationship with the other party.

11. Summarize and Confirm Agreement:

Summarize key points and agreements reached during the negotiation.

Confirm understanding and consensus to ensure clarity and alignment before concluding the negotiation.

12. Follow-Up and Support:

Follow up with the other party after the negotiation to ensure satisfaction and address any additional needs.

Provide ongoing support and assistance as needed to maintain the relationship and foster goodwill.

Chapter 6: Closing the Deal

Recognizing buying signals is crucial for sales professionals as it indicates the customer's interest and readiness to make a purchase. These signals can be both verbal and non-verbal cues that suggest the customer is moving closer to a buying decision. By identifying and responding to these signals effectively, sales professionals can capitalize on the opportunity to close the sale. Here are some key buying signals to look out for:

1. Verbal Indicators:

Expressions of interest: Statements such as "I like this" or "Tell me more about this product/service" indicate the customer's interest in what you're offering.

Asking specific questions: When a customer asks about pricing, delivery options, or product features, it suggests they are considering making a purchase.

Seeking reassurance: Questions about warranties, guarantees, or return policies indicate the customer's desire to mitigate risk and ensure satisfaction with the purchase.

2. Non-Verbal Cues:

Body language: Positive body language, such as leaning forward, nodding, or making eye contact, suggests engagement and interest in the conversation.

Facial expressions: Smiling or nodding in agreement can indicate that the customer is receptive to your pitch and considering the offer seriously.

Physical proximity: If the customer moves closer to the product or lingers around a particular item, it may indicate a higher level of interest.

3. Emotional Responses:

Excitement: A customer's enthusiasm or excitement about a product or service suggests they are emotionally invested and may be ready to buy.

Relatability: If the customer shares personal anecdotes or connects emotionally with the benefits of the product/service, it indicates a strong affinity and potential for purchase.

4. Intent to Purchase:

Making commitments: Statements like "I think this is exactly what I need" or "When can I get started?" signal the customer's readiness to move forward with the purchase.

Discussing logistics: If the customer starts discussing logistics, such as delivery dates or installation requirements, it indicates they are planning for the purchase.

5. Repeat Visits or Interactions:

Returning for multiple visits: If a customer returns to your store or website multiple times to inquire about a product/service, it suggests they are seriously considering the purchase.

Engaging in follow-up communication: If the customer responds positively to follow-up calls, emails, or messages, it indicates continued interest and potential for conversion.

6. Asking for Recommendations or Referrals:

Seeking validation: If the customer asks for recommendations or referrals from satisfied customers, it suggests they are seeking reassurance and validation before making a decision.

Involving others:

If the customer involves others, such as friends or family members, in the decision-making process, it indicates they value their opinions and may be close to making a purchase.

7. Expressing Urgency:

Time-sensitive requests: If the customer expresses a sense of urgency or requests expedited service, it suggests they are motivated to make a purchase quickly.

Mentioning deadlines: If the customer mentions upcoming deadlines or events that require the product or service, it indicates a need for timely action.

Overcoming final objections

Overcoming final objections is a critical step in the sales process that can make the difference between closing a deal and losing a sale. Final objections often arise when a customer is on the verge of making a decision but still has lingering concerns or hesitations. By addressing these objections effectively, sales professionals can remove barriers to purchase and secure a successful outcome. Here are some strategies for overcoming final objections:

1. Active Listening:

Listen attentively to the customer's objections without interrupting or rushing to respond.

Demonstrate empathy and understanding by acknowledging their concerns and validating their perspective.

2. Clarify the Objection:

Ask clarifying questions to gain a deeper understanding of the customer's objection.

Seek to uncover the underlying reasons behind their hesitation and address them directly.

3. Provide Reassurance:

Offer reassurance by highlighting the benefits and value of your product or service.

Emphasize how your offering addresses the customer's specific needs and concerns.

4. Address Misconceptions:

Correct any misconceptions or misunderstandings the customer may have about your product or service.

Provide clear and accurate information to alleviate their concerns and build trust.

5. Offer Solutions:

Propose solutions or alternatives to address the customer's objections.

Tailor your responses to meet their needs and preferences, demonstrating flexibility and a willingness to accommodate their concerns.

6. Provide Social Proof:

Share testimonials, case studies, or success stories from satisfied customers who have faced similar objections.

Use social proof to validate the effectiveness and reliability of your offering.

7. Address Risk:

Address any perceived risks or uncertainties that are holding the customer back from making a decision.

Offer guarantees, warranties, or trial periods to mitigate risk and provide peace of mind.

8. Close with Confidence:

Maintain a confident and positive demeanor throughout the conversation.

Express conviction in the value and benefits of your product or service, inspiring confidence in the customer's decision.

9. Negotiate if Necessary:

Be prepared to negotiate terms or concessions to overcome the customer's objections.

Find mutually agreeable solutions that meet both parties' needs and facilitate closing the deal.

10. Follow-Up and Support:

Offer ongoing support and assistance to address any remaining concerns or questions the customer may have.

Follow up after addressing the objection to ensure their satisfaction and facilitate a smooth transition to closing the sale.

Asking for the Sale

Asking for the sale is a critical step in the sales process that requires confidence, clarity, and timing. While it may seem straightforward, many sales professionals hesitate or fail to explicitly ask for the sale, missing out on opportunities to close deals. Here are some tricks for effectively asking for the sale:

1. Be Direct and Assertive:

Clearly and confidently ask for the sale without beating around the bush or being ambiguous.

Use assertive language such as "Would you like to proceed with the purchase?" or "Are you ready to move forward today?"

2. Provide Value Reinforcement:

Remind the customer of the value and benefits of your product or service before asking for the sale.

Emphasize how your offering addresses their needs and solves their problems, reinforcing their decision to buy.

3. Offer a Call to Action:

Provide a clear call to action that prompts the customer to take the next step in the buying process.

For example, you can say, "Let's finalize the details today," or "Shall we go ahead and place the order?"

4. Overcome Remaining Objections:

Address any final objections or concerns the customer may have before asking for the sale.

Proactively resolve any remaining hesitations to remove barriers to purchase.

5. Create a Sense of Urgency:

Encourage the customer to act now by creating a sense of urgency or scarcity.

Highlight limited-time offers, promotions, or product availability to motivate immediate action.

6. Provide Assurances:

Offer reassurances to alleviate any lingering doubts or uncertainties the customer may have.

Provide guarantees, warranties, or satisfaction policies to mitigate risk and build trust.

7. Offer Incentives:

Sweeten the deal by offering incentives or bonuses to encourage the customer to make a purchase.

For example, you can offer discounts, free shipping, or complimentary upgrades as a way to add value and incentivize the sale.

8. Listen and Respond Accordingly:

Pay attention to the customer's verbal and non-verbal cues to gauge their readiness to buy.

Adjust your approach based on their responses and be prepared to address any final concerns or objections.

9. Assume the Close:

Approach the conversation with the mindset that the sale is already made, and you're simply guiding the customer through the final steps.

Project confidence and certainty in your ability to meet the customer's needs and deliver value.

10. Follow Up and Support:

After asking for the sale, be prepared to facilitate the transaction smoothly and provide any additional support or assistance the customer may need.

Follow up after the sale to ensure satisfaction and foster a positive post-purchase experience.

Chapter 7: Post-Sale Follow-Up

Customer satisfaction is paramount in today's business landscape, serving as a cornerstone for long-term success and growth. It refers to the degree to which customers are content with their interactions, experiences, and purchases from a company. Customer satisfaction is of utmost importance because of the following reasons:

1. Retention and Loyalty:

Satisfied customers are more likely to remain loyal to a brand, leading to increased customer retention rates.

Loyal customers not only continue to purchase from the company but also serve as brand advocates, promoting the business to others through positive word-of-mouth.

2. Repeat Business:

Satisfied customers are inclined to make repeat purchases and become regular patrons of the business.

Repeat business leads to higher customer lifetime value, as customers continue to generate revenue over an extended period.

3. Positive Reviews and Referrals:

Satisfied customers are more likely to leave positive reviews and recommendations, contributing to a company's reputation and credibility.

Word-of-mouth referrals from satisfied customers are highly influential and can attract new customers to the business.

4. Competitive Advantage:

Customer satisfaction can serve as a competitive differentiator, setting a company apart from competitors in the marketplace.

Businesses that prioritize customer satisfaction can gain a competitive edge by offering superior products, services, and experiences.

5. Reduced Churn and Complaints:

Satisfied customers are less likely to churn or switch to competitors, reducing customer turnover rates.

By addressing customer needs and concerns proactively, businesses can minimize complaints and negative feedback.

6. Increased Revenue and Profitability:

Satisfied customers contribute to increased revenue and profitability through repeat purchases, referrals, and positive brand associations.

Happy customers are willing to pay premium prices for products or services they perceive as valuable, leading to higher margins and profitability.

7. Brand Reputation and Trust:

Customer satisfaction enhances a company's brand reputation and fosters trust among consumers.

A positive reputation for delivering quality products and exceptional service attracts new customers and strengthens existing relationships.

8. Improved Employee Morale:

Satisfied customers have a positive impact on employee morale and job satisfaction.

Employees feel a sense of pride and fulfillment when they see the positive impact of their work on customer satisfaction levels.

9. Valuable Feedback and Insights:

Satisfied customers are more likely to provide valuable feedback and insights that can help improve products, services, and processes.

Customer feedback serves as a valuable source of information for identifying areas of improvement and innovation.

10. Sustainable Growth:

Customer satisfaction is essential for sustainable business growth and longevity.

By prioritizing customer satisfaction, companies can build a loyal customer base and create enduring relationships that support continued success over time.

Building Long Term Relationship

Building long-term relationships with customers is essential for sustained success and growth in any business. Long-term relationships not only lead to repeat business but also foster loyalty, advocacy, and positive word-of-mouth referrals. Here are some key strategies for building and nurturing long-term relationships with customers:

1. Establish Trust:

Trust is the foundation of any successful relationship. Build trust by delivering on promises, being transparent, and acting with integrity in all interactions.

2. Prioritize Communication:

Maintain regular and open communication with customers to stay top-of-mind and demonstrate your commitment to their satisfaction.

Listen actively to their feedback, concerns, and suggestions, and respond promptly and empathetically.

3. Provide Value:

Offer products, services, and experiences that provide tangible value and address the needs and preferences of your customers.

Go above and beyond to exceed their expectations and create memorable experiences.

4. Personalize Interactions:

Treat each customer as an individual with unique preferences and preferences.

Personalize your communications, offers, and recommendations based on their past interactions, purchase history, and demographics.

5. Be Responsive and Supportive:

Be accessible and responsive to customer inquiries, requests, and concerns.

Provide timely and helpful support to address issues and ensure a positive resolution.

6. Show Appreciation:

Express gratitude to customers for their business and loyalty.

Offer special discounts, rewards, or exclusive perks as a token of appreciation for their continued support.

7. Build Emotional Connections:

Connect with customers on an emotional level by understanding their values, aspirations, and challenges.

Share authentic stories, engage in meaningful conversations, and demonstrate empathy and understanding.

8. Seek Feedback and Act on It:

Solicit feedback from customers through surveys, reviews, or direct conversations.

Use customer feedback to identify areas for improvement and make necessary adjustments to enhance the customer experience.

9. Foster Transparency and Accountability:

Be transparent about your products, services, pricing, and policies to build credibility and trust.

Take ownership of mistakes or shortcomings and work to rectify them promptly and transparently.

10. Stay Committed to Continuous Improvement:

Continuously strive to improve your products, services, and processes based on customer feedback and market trends.

Adapt to evolving customer needs and preferences to ensure ongoing relevance and value.

11. Invest in Relationship-Building Activities:

Organize events, webinars, or customer appreciation programs to foster connections and strengthen relationships.

Engage with customers on social media platforms, forums, or community groups to build a sense of belonging and camaraderie.

12. Measure and Monitor Customer Satisfaction:

Use customer satisfaction metrics, such as Net Promoter Score (NPS) or customer satisfaction surveys, to measure the health of your relationships.

Monitor trends over time and take proactive steps to address any declines in satisfaction or loyalty.

Asking for referrals and testimonials

Asking for referrals and testimonials is a powerful way to leverage satisfied customers to generate new business and build credibility for your brand. Referrals and testimonials serve as social proof of your company's value and quality, making them invaluable assets in your marketing and sales efforts. You can to ask for referrals and testimonials:

1. Provide Exceptional Service:

The first step in generating referrals and testimonials is to consistently deliver exceptional service and value to your customers.

Satisfied customers are more likely to refer others and provide positive testimonials about their experiences.

2. Timing is Key:

Ask for referrals and testimonials at the right moment, when the customer's satisfaction is at its peak.

This could be immediately after a successful transaction, upon receiving positive feedback, or after resolving a customer's issue effectively.

3. Personalize Your Request:

Tailor your request for referrals and testimonials to each individual customer.

Personalized requests show that you value their opinion and are more likely to elicit a positive response.

4. Be Clear and Specific:

Clearly explain what you're asking for and why it's important.

Specify whether you're seeking referrals, testimonials, or both, and provide guidance on what information or format you're looking for.

5. Express Appreciation:

Express gratitude for the customer's business and loyalty before making your request.

Let them know that their feedback and referrals are valuable and appreciated.

6. Make It Easy:

Remove barriers and make it as easy as possible for customers to provide referrals and testimonials.

Provide clear instructions and convenient methods for submitting referrals or testimonials, such as online forms or email templates.

7. Incentivize if Appropriate:

Consider offering incentives or rewards for customers who provide referrals or testimonials.

This could be in the form of discounts, freebies, or exclusive offers as a token of appreciation for their support.

8. Follow Up:

If a customer agrees to provide a referral or testimonial, follow up promptly to collect the information.

Be persistent but respectful in your follow-up efforts, and provide any assistance or guidance they may need.

9. Showcase Testimonials:

Once you've collected testimonials, showcase them prominently on your website, social media channels, and marketing materials.

Positive testimonials build trust and credibility with prospective customers and reinforce your brand's reputation.

10. Act on Referrals:

Follow up promptly on referrals provided by existing customers.

Reach out to referred leads with personalized messages and offer exceptional service to convert them into customers.

11. Say Thank You:

Always express gratitude to customers who provide referrals and testimonials.

A simple thank-you note or gesture goes a long way in nurturing relationships and encouraging future engagement.

Chapter 8: Adapting to Different Industries and Markets

Understanding market trends and dynamics is essential for businesses to stay competitive, anticipate changes, and capitalize on emerging opportunities. Market trends refer to the general direction in which a market is moving, while market dynamics encompass the forces and factors that influence these trends. So, understanding market trends and dynamics is crucial:

1. Anticipating Customer Needs:

By analyzing market trends, businesses can gain insights into changing customer preferences, behaviors, and demands.

Anticipating customer needs allows businesses to develop products, services, and marketing strategies that resonate with their target audience.

2. Identifying Growth Opportunities:

Market trends can highlight emerging growth sectors, niches, or market segments that offer potential opportunities for expansion.

By identifying these opportunities early, businesses can position themselves to capitalize on them and gain a competitive advantage.

3. Mitigating Risks:

Understanding market dynamics enables businesses to identify potential risks, threats, and challenges that may impact their operations.

By staying informed about market conditions, businesses can develop proactive strategies to mitigate risks and minimize their impact on performance.

4. Strategic Decision-Making:

Market trends and dynamics provide valuable data and insights that inform strategic decision-making at all levels of the organization.

From product development and pricing strategies to marketing initiatives and expansion plans, businesses can align their decisions with market realities to drive success.

5. Competitive Analysis:

Analyzing market trends allows businesses to assess their competitive landscape and benchmark themselves against industry peers.

By understanding competitors' strengths, weaknesses, and strategies, businesses can identify areas for differentiation and develop competitive advantages.

6. Innovation and Adaptation:

Market trends often signal shifts in consumer preferences, technological advancements, or regulatory changes that require businesses to innovate and adapt.

Businesses that stay ahead of the curve by innovating and adapting to changing market dynamics are better positioned for long-term success.

7. Enhancing Customer Experience:

Market trends provide insights into evolving customer expectations and the factors that influence their purchasing decisions.

By aligning their strategies with market trends, businesses can enhance the customer experience and build stronger relationships with their audience.

8. Maximizing Return on Investment (ROI):

By investing resources in areas aligned with market trends and dynamics, businesses can maximize their return on investment.

Strategic allocation of resources ensures that businesses focus their efforts on initiatives that are most likely to drive growth and profitability.

9. Regulatory Compliance:

Market trends include regulatory changes, industry standards, and compliance requirements that businesses must navigate.

Staying abreast of regulatory developments helps businesses ensure compliance and avoid penalties or reputational damage.

10. Continuous Learning and Improvement:

Understanding market trends and dynamics requires continuous learning and monitoring of industry developments.

By staying curious, adaptable, and open-minded, businesses can foster a culture of learning and continuous improvement that drives innovation and success.

Customizing Sales Approaches to Different Audiences

Tailoring sales approaches to different audiences is crucial for effectively engaging with diverse groups of customers, each with unique preferences, needs, and priorities. By understanding the characteristics and preferences of different audience segments, sales professionals can personalize their approach to resonate with each group effectively. Here's how to tailor sales approaches to different audiences:

1. Segment Your Audience:

Divide your target audience into distinct segments based on demographics, psychographics, behavior, or other relevant criteria.

Common segmentation variables include age, gender, income, occupation, geographic location, interests, and purchasing behavior.

2. Understand Audience Preferences:

Conduct market research and analysis to gain insights into the preferences, motivations, and pain points of each audience segment.

Use surveys, interviews, customer feedback, and data analytics to gather information about their needs, expectations, and buying behaviors.

3. Customize Messaging and Communication:

Tailor your messaging and communication style to resonate with the preferences and communication preferences of each audience segment.

Use language, tone, and imagery that appeal to their interests, values, and aspirations.

4. Highlight Relevant Benefits and Solutions:

Identify the specific benefits and solutions that are most relevant and compelling to each audience segment.

Highlight how your product or service addresses their unique needs, solves their problems, and provides value.

5. Adapt Sales Techniques and Strategies:

Adjust your sales techniques and strategies to accommodate the preferences and buying behaviors of different audience segments.

For example, some segments may respond better to consultative selling, while others may prefer a more direct and transactional approach.

6. Offer Personalized Recommendations:

Provide personalized recommendations and solutions based on the specific needs and preferences of each audience segment.

Demonstrate that you understand their challenges and can offer tailored solutions that meet their requirements.

7. Use Multiple Channels and Touch-points:

Reach each audience segment through their preferred channels and touch-points, such as email, social media, phone calls, or in-person meetings.

Build an omni channel sales approach that allows customers to engage with your brand seamlessly across different platforms.

8. Adjust Pricing and Promotions:

Customize pricing and promotional offers to align with the budget constraints and purchasing behavior of each audience segment.

Offer discounts, incentives, or bundle deals that appeal to their specific needs and preferences.

9. Provide Exceptional Customer Service:

Deliver personalized and responsive customer service that meets the expectations of each audience segment.

Anticipate their needs, address their concerns promptly, and go the extra mile to exceed their expectations.

10. Continuously Evaluate and Refine:

Regularly review and analyze the effectiveness of your sales approaches with different audience segments.

Collect feedback, monitor performance metrics, and iterate on your strategies to optimize results and improve engagement over time.

Conclusion

Let's recap the key points:

Segment Your Audience: Divide your target audience into distinct segments based on demographics, psychographics, behavior, or other relevant criteria.

Understand Audience Preferences: Conduct market research and analysis to gain insights into the preferences, motivations, and pain points of each audience segment.

Customize Messaging and Communication: Tailor your messaging and communication style to resonate with the preferences and communication preferences of each audience segment.

Highlight Relevant Benefits and Solutions: Identify the specific benefits and solutions that are most relevant and compelling to each audience segment.

Adapt Sales Techniques and Strategies: Adjust your sales techniques and strategies to accommodate the preferences and buying behaviors of different audience segments.

Offer Personalized Recommendations: Provide personalized recommendations and solutions based on the specific needs and preferences of each audience segment.

Use Multiple Channels and Touchpoints: Reach each audience segment through their preferred channels and touchpoints, such as email, social media, phone calls, or in-person meetings.

Adjust Pricing and Promotions: Customize pricing and promotional offers to align with the budget constraints and purchasing behavior of each audience segment.

Provide Exceptional Customer Service: Deliver personalized and responsive customer service that meets the expectations of each audience segment.

Continuously Evaluate and Refine: Regularly review and analyze the effectiveness of your sales approaches with different audience segments and iterate on your strategies to optimize results.

Some Case Studies

Case Study 1: Improving Sales Performance with Personalization

Background:

A software-as-a-service (SaaS) company was struggling to meet its sales targets due to stiff competition and a lack of differentiation in the market. Despite having a high-quality product, the company found it challenging to stand out and win new customers.

Challenge:

The company recognized the need to personalize its sales approach to better resonate with its target audience and differentiate itself from competitors. They wanted to improve their sales performance by understanding customer needs more effectively and tailoring their messaging and solutions accordingly.

Solution:

The company implemented a personalized sales strategy that involved:

Segmenting their target audience based on industry, company size, and pain points.

Conducting in-depth research to understand the unique needs and challenges of each segment.

Customizing their sales pitches and presentations to address specific pain points and offer tailored solutions.

Leveraging personalized follow-up emails and communications to maintain engagement and build rapport with prospects.

Results:

By implementing a personalized sales approach, the company achieved significant improvements in sales performance:

Increased conversion rates: By addressing specific pain points and offering tailored solutions, the company saw a noticeable increase in conversion rates among their target audience.

Higher customer satisfaction: Customers appreciated the personalized approach and felt that the company understood their needs better, resulting in higher satisfaction levels and stronger relationships.

Improved competitive advantage: The company was able to differentiate itself from competitors by offering personalized solutions that directly addressed customer pain points, giving them a competitive edge in the market.

Case Study 2: Leveraging Data Analytics to Drive Sales Growth

Background:

A retail company was struggling to drive sales growth in a highly competitive market. They had a large customer base but lacked insights into customer behavior and preferences, making it challenging to target their marketing and sales efforts effectively.

Challenge:

The company needed a way to leverage data analytics to gain a deeper understanding of customer behavior and preferences. They wanted to use data-driven insights to identify opportunities for cross-selling, upselling, and personalized marketing campaigns to drive sales growth.

Solution:

The company implemented a data analytics solution that involved:

Collecting and analyzing customer data from various sources, including transaction records, website interactions, and social media engagement.

Using advanced analytics techniques, such as predictive modeling and segmentation analysis, to identify patterns, trends, and correlations in the data.

Generating actionable insights into customer preferences, purchase behavior, and product affinities.

Leveraging these insights to develop targeted marketing campaigns, personalized product recommendations, and sales strategies tailored to individual customer segments.

Results:

By leveraging data analytics to drive sales growth, the company achieved remarkable results:

Increased revenue: By targeting customers with personalized offers and recommendations, the company saw a significant increase in sales and revenue.

Improved customer satisfaction: Customers appreciated the personalized shopping experience and were more likely to make repeat purchases, leading to higher satisfaction levels and increased loyalty.

Enhanced marketing effectiveness: By targeting marketing campaigns based on data-driven insights, the company achieved higher conversion rates and return on investment for their marketing efforts.

Competitive advantage: The company gained a competitive edge by leveraging data analytics to better understand customer needs and preferences, allowing them to outperform competitors and capture market share.

These case studies demonstrate the power of personalized sales approaches and data analytics in driving sales growth and achieving competitive advantage in today's marketplace. By leveraging these strategies effectively, businesses can unlock new opportunities for growth, improve customer satisfaction, and stay ahead of the competition.

Dear Reader,

Congratulations on taking the first step towards mastering the art of sales! You've invested your time and energy into learning valuable techniques and strategies that have the power to transform your sales game and propel you towards unprecedented success.

But remember, knowledge alone isn't enough to reach your goals. It's the action you take that truly sets you apart and paves the way for greatness. Now is the time to harness the power of what you've learned and unleash it into the world.

Imagine the possibilities that await you when you confidently apply these sales techniques in your interactions with prospects and customers. Picture yourself closing deals with ease, building strong relationships, and exceeding your sales targets beyond imagination.

Yes, the journey may not always be easy. There will be challenges, setbacks, and moments of doubt along the way. But it's precisely in those moments that your true strength and resilience shine through. Every obstacle you overcome brings you one step closer to your dreams.

You have within you the potential to achieve greatness in sales and beyond. Believe in yourself, trust in your abilities, and never underestimate the impact you can make.

So, let today be the day you decide to take action. Seize every opportunity that comes your way, embrace every challenge as a chance to grow, and never stop striving for excellence.

The world is waiting for your brilliance, your passion, and your unique contribution. Step into your greatness, unleash your potential, and let your sales success reach to new heights!

You've got this!

Warm regards,

Asit Saha

Appendix: Additional Resources and Tools

In this appendix, you'll find a curated list of additional resources and tools to further enhance your sales knowledge and skills. These resources cover a wide range of topics, including sales techniques, communication strategies, customer relationship management, and personal development. Whether you are a matured sales professional or just starting in the field, these resources can provide valuable insights, tips, and inspiration to support your growth and success in sales.

1. Books:

"To Sell is Human: The Surprising Truth About Moving Others" by Daniel H. Pink

"SPIN Selling" by Neil Rackham

"Influence: The Psychology of Persuasion" by Robert Cialdini

"How to Win Friends and Influence People" by Dale Carnegie

"The Challenger Sale: Taking Control of the Customer Conversation" by Matthew Dixon and Brent Adamson

2. Online Courses and Training Programs:

LinkedIn Learning: Offers a wide range of sales courses, including sales techniques, negotiation skills, and customer relationship management.

Coursera: Provides courses from top universities and institutions on topics such as sales strategies, sales management, and business development.

Udemy: Features a diverse selection of sales courses taught by industry experts, covering everything from prospecting to closing techniques.

3. Podcasts:

"The Advanced Selling Podcast" hosted by Bill Caskey and Bryan Neale: Offers practical advice and strategies for improving sales performance.

"The Sales Evangelist" hosted by Donald C. Kelly: Provides insights and interviews with sales professionals to help listeners master the art of selling.

"Sell or Die" hosted by Jeffrey Gitomer and Jennifer Gitomer: Offers motivational sales tips, strategies, and success stories to inspire sales professionals.

4. Software and Tools:

Salesforce: A leading customer relationship management (CRM) platform that helps businesses manage sales pipelines, track leads, and automate sales processes.

HubSpot Sales: Offers a suite of sales tools, including email tracking, meeting scheduling, and contact management, to streamline sales workflows.

LinkedIn Sales Navigator: Provides advanced prospecting and lead generation capabilities to help sales professionals identify and connect with potential customers on LinkedIn.

5. Blogs and Websites:

Sales Hacker: Features articles, guides, and resources on sales techniques, strategies, and best practices.

Gong.io Blog: Offers insights and analysis based on data from sales calls and conversations to help improve sales performance.

SalesGravy: Provides sales training, coaching, and resources for sales professionals at all levels.

6. Networking and Community:

Join professional networking groups on LinkedIn and other social media platforms to connect with fellow sales professionals, share insights, and learn from others' experiences.

Attend industry events, conferences, and workshops to network with peers, gain new perspectives, and stay updated on the latest trends and innovations in sales.

These resources are just a starting point on your journey to sales excellence. Continuously seek out new opportunities for learning, growth, and development to stay ahead in the competitive world of sales. Remember, success in sales is not just about what you know but how you apply that knowledge to achieve meaningful results.

Don't miss out!

Visit the website below and you can sign up to receive emails whenever Asit Saha publishes a new book. There's no charge and no obligation.

https://books2read.com/r/B-A-WRTEB-JDZZC

BOOKS 2 READ

Connecting independent readers to independent writers.

Did you love *Mastering Sales: Strategies for Winning Deals*? Then you should read *Unlocking Business Opportunities For Students*[1] by Asit Saha!

[2]

"Unlocking Business Opportunities for Students" is a comprehensive guide designed to empower aspiring student entrepreneurs to navigate the complexities of starting and growing their own businesses while balancing academic commitments. From refining business ideas to scaling ventures, this guide provides practical insights, strategies, and resources tailored specifically for students embarking on the entrepreneurial journey.

The guide begins by emphasizing the importance of identifying business opportunities aligned with personal interests, skills, and market demand. Through market research, prototyping, and testing, students

---

1. https://books2read.com/u/3L8ree

2. https://books2read.com/u/3L8ree

learn to validate their ideas and develop unique value propositions that resonate with target customers.

Students are then guided through the process of crafting comprehensive business plans, setting SMART goals, and establishing ethical business practices. Financial planning, budgeting, and understanding legal and intellectual property requirements are highlighted as essential components for success.

Recognizing the challenges faced by student entrepreneurs, the guide offers strategies for overcoming obstacles, managing time effectively, and balancing academic and entrepreneurial commitments. Students are encouraged to seek mentorship, leverage networking opportunities, and engage with entrepreneurship organizations to support their journey.

Practical advice is provided on launching and marketing startups, acquiring customers, and scaling businesses while managing academic responsibilities. Real-world case studies and success stories inspire and illustrate key concepts, while recommended books, websites, and online courses offer additional learning resources.

In conclusion, "Unlocking Business Opportunities for Students" serves as a roadmap for students to transform their entrepreneurial aspirations into tangible realities. By fostering creativity, resilience, and a growth mindset, this guide empowers students to unlock their potential, seize opportunities, and make a meaningful impact in the world of entrepreneurship.

About the Author

Writes to motivate and entertain.

* 9 7 9 8 2 2 4 7 2 4 9 4 9 *